ALL PRAISE BELONGS TO GOD

Other Works by James A Stump

<u>Walks Along the Pier:</u>
<u>Tales of a Wounded Healer</u>
A novel about the counseling profession

<u>Psychotherapy: All the Dirty Little Secrets Your Therapist Doesn't Want You To Know</u>
A guide to selecting your personal psychotherapist!

<u>Inspirational Stories:</u>
<u>Christmas Oranges</u>
<u>Douglas</u>
<u>Judah's Coming</u>
<u>The Seventh King</u>

<u>Christmas Threes</u>
Three short vignettes for the stage:
<u>The Christmas Thief</u>
<u>Christmas Neighbors</u>
<u>A Christmas Vignette</u>

Counselor's Couch

THE WOUNDED HEALER

Fiction

By

JAMES A STUMP

Licensed Marriage & Family Therapist

NOTICE:

This is a work of fiction.
Names, characters, places and incidents
are either the product of the author's imagination
or are used fictitiously
and any resemblance to actual persons living or
dead, events, or locales is entirely coincidental.

The content of this book was previously published
in: <u>Walks Along the Pier</u>.

No part of this book may be reproduced, stored in
a retrieval system, or transmitted by any means,
electronic, mechanical, photocopying, recording,
or otherwise, without written permission from the
author.

Copyright 2014 by James A Stump, LMFT
All Rights Reserved.

ISBN13: 9781500785338
ISBN10: 1500785334

Cover & book design by
GBSPublishing/Graphics

The Wounded Healer

There is an oft told story in the counseling professions - the Legend of the Wounded Healer. The story originated in Greek Mythology but modern versions are told something like this.

Long ago in a faraway land during a great war, a physician stood on the side of the battle and watched his countrymen fall in the fierce fighting. Hearing their cries of pain and suffering, the physician could bear it no longer. He ran out onto the field and began ministering to the wounded. Binding a cut here, removing an arrow there, he provided solace and comfort to every soldier whose pain he attended.

The enemy, seeing the physician, began to train their weapons on him and the more they struck him, the better his healing became. As he moved from fallen brother to brother, solider to hero, to those afraid of dying, the men to whom he ministered said that his work was near miraculous.

While the enemy continually sought to bring down the physician, he stopped at one soldier and swiftly and efficiently tended to his wounds. The soldier in awe and gratitude said to the healer, "Thank you, brother. Your work is so good. How is it that you know just where to apply your ministrations?"

"Simple," murmured the healer. "I know where it hurts."

*

"Judging from all the stories you've told me, it seems you want to complain about your job."

"Yeah… I guess so…"

"So, let me ask you. Are you a 'rescuer'? What kind of psychotherapy do you practice?"

"Humanistic, client-centered, Rogerian... Psycho-antisocial, pseudo dynamic...psycho-neuro-pathetic. The usual."

"And...uh...this 'creative' approach didn't work with that last client?"

"...I sort of lost it..."

"How did you 'lose it'?"

"Uh... I let my personal feelings get involved with my work."

"Tell me about that."

"Well, it's...hard to explain. One minute I was doing fine and the next she was screaming at me."

"It sounds like *she* 'lost it.' Why do you think *you* did something wrong?"

"Uh... I said the wrong thing. She wasn't ready. I offended her."

"Was it intentional? Or did you stumble on one of her triggers?"

"Both, I'm sure. We were in a restaurant...Austin's over here on the pier. I'm sure you know it."

"Hmm. Yes, I know it."

"And this woman just attacked me – verbally. I was unable to work her through it."

"Why couldn't you work through it?"

"...uh... 'Cause she stood up, loudly denigrated all men and stormed out of the place before I could get my foot out of my mouth."

"Do you think that she needed to get it out? To say what she said?"

"Yes, I do. But that wasn't the right time or place to say it."

"We'll get back to that. What do you think you said that was wrong?"

"Uh... Basically I told her that she was re-enacting her family of origin emotional rejection in her unsuccessful relationships with men."

"Had you known her long?"

"First meeting."

"Then why on earth did you make that interpretation?"

"Based on what she had told me, her emotional cut-off from her parents, her lack of successful personal relationship, her dismissive treatment of me and the waiters, and her self-disclosed absence of trust in her employees and other cues."

"At the time did you feel your interpretation was accurate?"

"Yes."

"And now on reflection what do you think about the exchange?"

"Hmmm... I think the interpretation was accurate but the presentation was a mite faulty."

"What was faulty about the presentation?"

"I used a Phase Two interpretation when I should have been building a Phase One connection with the client."

"To say the least. Instead of 'making an interpretation', why didn't you just back up, reframe and re-connect with your client?"

"I'm not sure. I didn't think of it at the time."

"Why not?"

"By then she was screaming at me. I was fumbling over my words. People were gawking.

You know – the usual public restaurant humiliation type of counseling blunder that we've all had."

"I see. Let me ask you this. Was your 'interpretation' judgmental?"

"…'judgmental?'… What do you mean?"

"Were you trying to make her feel bad about herself? Trying to make her feel 'wrong'?"

"Hmm…maybe so… How would I know I was doing that?"

"How would you…? Let's put it another way. How do you feel about your clients?"

"How do I *feel* about my clients? Now, what does *that* mean?"

"I mean, do you like your clients? Do you not like them? Do they annoy you? Do you resent them? Have you grown tired of the work? Are they just paychecks?"

"That's an awful lot of negative choices, doctor!"

"All right. Do you *love* your clients? Do you look forward to seeing them? Are you fascinated by the work?"

"Ha! No. No. But, ah...they're definitely not pay checks. Hmm... I think...on some level...I resent them. ...yes... I think that's ...that's got something to do with how I feel."

"Why do you resent them?"

"Well... You know... They impose on you. Beyond what they have a right to. They demand extra time and attention. And emotional energy. Then a lot of them don't give anything back."

"Give anything back? Professional services are exchanged for professional fees. What *else* would you want them to 'give back'?"

"Aaah, well... I think we'd better leave *that* subject alone."

"What subject?"

"...the subject of fees..."

"All right. For the moment. Then tell me more about how they impose on you."

"You know, that's funny. Lately they just show up and expect me to drop everything and be there waiting for them. Why do you suppose they do that? Do I have the word 'sucker' painted on my forehead?"

"Do you hold appropriate boundaries with that kind of behavior?"

"No. I guess I don't."

"Maybe that's why they do it."

"…yeah…maybe…"

"You said something about 'giving back'. Some of them do? Give something back?"

"Yeah. I have to admit…some of them do."

"What do they give back?"

"Uhm… Human connection, I think. I guess that's the best way to describe it. Some of them connect with whatever is bothering them and then they open up… They get it. They learn something about themselves and they improve. That's a fascinating change to watch. And it's a privilege to be a part of it. For me, that's 'giving back.' It means my work was successful."

"Human connection?"

"Huh?"

"You said, 'human connection.' For you counseling is human connection? Don't you have a social life?"

"...yeah. Sure I do..."

"Tell me about your social life."

"All right. So I *don't* have much of a social life. ...Thanks, doc. Keep rubbing it in."

"I wasn't trying to. Okay, then. How is it a privilege to work with your clients?"

"You're in the counseling profession. You should know what I mean."

"I want to hear *you* say it. I want to know how *you* experience it."

"Uh... It's hard to describe. When a person opens up, they are vulnerable. That means they trust you, trust that you won't hurt them. Not that they think it's not going to be painful but...they trust that it's going to benefit them eventually. When they open up, you get to see the real person behind all of their defenses. And that's always beautiful. You...or at least I...can't help but be attracted to a real person. It's what I've tried to teach all my clients – that when they open up and become honest with the other people in their lives, relationships improve. People understand each other. They like each other better. Most people are afraid that their honesty will make them vulnerable – open to attack. That's why they stay defended."

"If they are honest and open up, *are* they more vulnerable?"

"Sometimes, yes. But anyone who uses your honesty against you has revealed *their* personal shortcomings, not yours. It's not that you have to stop being honest. It's just that...you know what kind of person the other person is so you know how to deal with them. You know how *much* you can trust them – and to what degree. So no matter *how* a person's honesty is received, it works out for the best in the end. *That's* what I try to teach my clients. So...where were we?"

"You were telling me how you felt about your work as a counselor. And I was getting the impression that you like working with people."

"Yeah. People are fascinating. Human behavior is the most interesting phenomenon to study."

"But apparently your work in counseling has had its…what should we call it? A down side?"

"Yes. It has."

"And what is that down side?"

"Uh… People blame you for decisions *they've* made. You're just trying to help and they…fight like hell over therapy things."

"What kind of therapy things?"

"Uhm… The defenses you point out. And the dysfunctional behavior you accurately identify. If they're not open and ready to explore their own contributions to their problems, they hate that and they deny everything."

"Like the lady at Austin's."

"Yeah… Like that. Dealing with client anger is really what counselors get paid for. The rest is fun – it's interesting! But their anger…gets difficult to take…at times…"

"You don't enjoy your clients' anger."

"No."

"It's not fun. It's not interesting."

"...no..."

"It hurts."

Silence.

"Let's explore another issue. How do you know you have 'identified their dysfunctional behavior accurately'?"

"Good question. Maybe that's part of my dilemma. Maybe I only *think* I have identified it accurately."

"Okay. But for the moment let's assume that you *have* identified their issues accurately. If you know that they're 'not open and ready to explore their own contributions to their problems' and that they 'hate that', why would you do it?"

"Why would I *do* it? Because I'm trying to help them! Identifying issues is how therapy works! I mean, I'm not *trying* to offend them – not usually, anyway. I try to be sensitive to the emotional place of the client. But sometimes you fail."

"How do you fail?"

"Oh... Sometimes you miscalculate, say something too early that they're not ready for, say it the wrong way. Or blurt something out that you shouldn't have said. Use humor ineffectively. Or just stumble onto one of their sore spots that you didn't know was there. People have lots of triggers – lots of unfinished emotional baggage that they carry around and blame the world for. And if you make that kind of an error, clients can be most unforgiving. They never forget what you said that hurt them. I've had clients I worked with for years who have held a grudge against me for something I said years before. Sometimes I instantly know I made a mistake. Other times I'm not even aware of it. But the client never forgets."

"Why do you suppose that is?"

"Because of that trust. They trusted you with something very personal, very private or painful to them and you either disrespected that trust or were oblivious as to how much that issue meant to the client. If they stay with the counseling, some clients work through those negative reactions and maybe even come to forgive you for being human. The best clients come to understand *how* you were trying to help them. Then they appreciate you. But a lot of them don't stay. They feel betrayed and they just don't come back. Maybe it's their way of showing their resentment against you. They vote with their feet. But the sad part is that they haven't addressed their issues. They haven't changed a thing and they've likely cemented their resentment even more. Which means that your counseling hasn't helped. And maybe it actually made them worse."

"How does that make you feel? When clients 'vote with their feet' and you imagine that 'your counseling has actually made them worse'?"

"Ha! Psychology 101? 'How does that make you *feel*?' You don't have anything better than that?"

"You can phrase the question anyway you like. But you know as well as I what I'm asking."

"Yes, I suppose I do. How does that make me feel? Betrayed."

"Betrayed? Who betrayed you?"

"I was betrayed by the profession. By the idea that training and experience in a therapist could facilitate insight in a client that could lead to change for the better. Some of that's not true. I can't make a client change anything. They have to make their own choices."

"You sound like a text book. Do you talk to your clients that way?"

"I try to mirror the client's linguistic style. I'll dumb it down for *you*."

"'Training and experience produce insight to induce an agreement for change.' Are you saying that therapy *doesn't* work like that?"

"I'm saying that *some* clients won't *let* it work like that even though it should. Clients expect a therapist to be perfect – to 'ease their pain' without *them* doing any work. To have just the right words in all situations to make their lives better without ever saying anything that offends them. They want the counselor to take *their* side and to teach them how to make *other* people change. Counselors can't be ordinary people. They're not allowed to make mistakes. There is no forgiveness with clients."

"Is that how you see counseling? That you have to be perfect and that you can never offend a client?"

"Pretty much. How do you see it?"

"I see that you're being very hard on yourself. Where did you get this need for perfection?"

"I didn't have alcoholic parents – not an alcoholic mother, at any rate – so don't go there."

"Okay. If not alcoholic, how about emotionally unavailable?"

"Don't go there, either."

"All right. But I want to state for the record so that we're both aware of it that that's the fourth issue you've refused to address."

"Just like a real client, huh. Okay. So noted for the record."

"Very well. I'll let you off for today but sooner or later you'll have to talk about these things with someone. But for now, let's go back to something safe for you. This idea of 'perfect counseling'. There are many ways to work with clients. And I'm sure you know a lot of them. Gestalt therapy – for example - asks the client to be very real and honest in each session. But if you 'never offend a client', how does the client gain the self-awareness you say you want for them?"

"Well, my preferred approach is to walk with them to their own understanding. My theory is that a client is more likely to gain self-awareness when they find it for themselves. I try to help them do that."

"Is that how it worked for you?'

"Ha! You know it is."

"And that's why you practice the way you do. It worked for you and you want to share your success with them."

"Yeah. The short answer is yes, that's how it worked for me and that's why I want to share it with others."

"Did it work for the lady at Austin's?"

Beat.

"…cute…"

"Is that what you're expecting from *this* session? That kind of person-centered, supportive, unconditional positive regard approach?"

"It wouldn't be unappreciated, I can tell you that!"

We both laughed. It feels nice to be able to share a joke with your therapist.

"How far does that approach take the counseling? And how much time does it require?"

"Okay. You got me there. Client centered counseling usually requires a bit of time. But the client feels comfortable with the journey. Some other approaches don't feel as…supportive. And if the client doesn't stay, the counseling wasn't successful anyway. So what good was *that* approach? Besides, I don't believe short term counseling has lasting effects. It takes a while to change the behaviors of a lifetime."

"So, is that what leads you to your feeling of being 'betrayed'? When you give all of that support to a client and the client doesn't appear to appreciate it?"

"...yeah. I guess that's it... A lot of it, anyway."

"What else is missing?"

"I don't know. I really don't. I haven't identified it yet."

"Okay. So, tell me again, how does *this* counseling feel to you? Is it what you were looking for?"

"So far. But I have a feeling you're going to beat me up sooner or later."

Another shared chuckle. An ominous, portentous chortle.

"Would that be so difficult? If this counseling 'beat you up'?"

"It would be like the last relationship I tried to have."

23

"And how was that? With an emotionally unavailable girlfriend who was like that alcoholic father and that emotionally unavailable mother you didn't want to talk about?"

"...yeah..."

"And so, if this counseling 'beat you up', it would feel like emotional abandonment?"

"...yeah...that's the way it would feel..."

"So, you need to *enjoy* counseling for it to be effective?"

"I don't know. We'll see."

"What do you think I could say that would be uncomfortable for you?"

"Huh-huh! It's *your* job to figure that out!"

"Humor me."

"Okay, uh... You could tell me that I'm a lousy counselor."

"*Are* you a lousy counselor?"

"I don't know. A lot of times, I feel that way. Not effective. I try to be a good counselor but...sometimes I don't think I make it."

"And what would make you think you sometimes are *not* an effective counselor?"

"Jeez! Are we going to spend this session cataloging my lack of skills and ability?"

"I don't know. Are we?"

"I would rather not!"

"*Why* not?"

"Because it makes me feel incompetent."

"*Are* you incompetent?"

"I don't think so!"

"Then why would you worry about that?"

She had me there. I didn't know how to respond. Without being painfully honest.

"Okay then, if you don't want to talk about your professional skills and abilities, your feelings of inadequacy in your profession, your family-of-origin abandonment issues, your social isolation, your sense of feeling 'used by your clients', what *would* you like to talk about?"

More silence. I didn't know *what* I was looking for. I didn't know what I was doing in a therapy session. I was as bad as the clients I complained about.

"May I make an observation?"

"You mean, an 'interpretation', don't you?"

She shrugged. "Okay. An 'interpretation'. May I make one?"

"Go for it." I said it but I didn't mean it. I wondered if she was aware of that.

"Let me phrase it as a question." Apparently she *was* aware of my trepidation. "How much of your sense of self-worth have you wrapped up in your success as a psychotherapist?"

"I don't even know what that means."

"Yes, you do."

I hate it when my counselor is right, don't you? Caught, trapped and exposed by my own words and honesty. No wonder clients defend themselves to the death.

"How much of my self-worth is wrapped up in my success as a psychotherapist? Under other circumstances, I might have said 'a moderate amount'. Under *these* circumstances…I would have to admit…I *hate* to fail."

"What does 'failure' mean to you?"

Funny as it seemed, I found myself pausing, not wanting to answer. Not wanting to *admit* the answer – not to another human being. I used to think I was *beyond* all that. That I had dealt with my personal issues at least to the point that I could work successfully as a therapist.

She waited. I waited. But the question did *not* go away.

"What does 'failure' mean to you?"

She repeated the question as though I might have forgotten it. In truth, I was doing my best to block it out of my mind. 'Failure' meant many things to me. Taunts from my childhood; recriminations from my adolescence; self-doubt from my training; failed relationships; self-blame from my professional practice. What did she want from me? Which one of those did she expect me to offer unto the altar of self-awareness?

"Pick one," she said. "You don't have to explore them all."

Reading my mind, was she? Was *that* how *my* clients felt when I did that to them?

"Uh…" I didn't want to explore the emotional degradation of my youth: it was too early in therapy for that. Which was to say that I didn't know her well enough to trust her with that information. I didn't want to acknowledge the shame of my adolescence – for the same reason: I didn't trust her with my embarrassment. Self-doubt from training was too obvious, trite and superficial. That left only… "Failure means that I haven't achieved the level of expertise I wanted in my chosen profession."

"This is where I came *in*," she told me. "We haven't moved an *inch*! What is it that you *don't* want to say?"

Lots of things. Too many things. Things I had hoped to leave buried. Could those *really* be the things that were bothering me and sinking my life in its current depression?

"There are many things I don't want to say. Are they relevant to what we're here for?"

"Everything you don't want to say is relevant."

"Don't pull those cheap counseling tricks on me. Please! I know them all and they aren't going to help."

She sat back; sighed. "Okay. No tricks. Then how *are* we supposed to proceed with this session?"

"*I* don't know. *You're* the one conducting it!"

"And *you're* the one obstructing it! How can counseling help you if you don't want to engage in it?"

Ah! The age-old question. The answer, apparently, was 'it couldn't help' if one resisted it. Wasn't *that* the complaint I had about *my* clients?

"If we're going to do *that*, don't we have to take off our pants first?"

I was deflecting her probe and I knew it. So did she.

"Only if we want to avoid doing the work. What does 'failure' mean to you?"

She was like a pit bull chomping at my private parts. I didn't appreciate it. But I understood it.

"Failure means 'I'm not doing my work well enough'."

"How well do you have to do your work before it's 'good enough'?"

She was teasing me. 'Good enough' was an expression taken from D. W. Winnicott's theory of the role of parenting in human development. In psychological communication it has come to mean that in order to be successful at some activity, a person's performance did not have to be 'perfect'; it only had to be 'more good than bad'. But 'good enough' wasn't good enough for me. Not for my work with other people. They deserved better than 'more good than bad'.

"It has to be 'good enough' that my clients benefit from talking with me."

"And what makes you think that they don't?"

Wounded Healer

I wasn't enjoying her relentless probing. This was our first session and already she was insisting that I trust her with all my insecurities. How could *any* client appreciate such intrusions into the limited self-esteem that held us together emotionally?

"I know when clients benefit and when they don't. Don't you?"

"*How* do you know that?"

"What does *that* mean? Anyone can tell when the person they're talking to is accepting or agreeing with what they're saying!"

"Is *that* your definition of success? When someone agrees with what you are saying?"

"You *know* that's not what I meant."

"I don't 'know' anything until you tell me. So, tell me! Why are you so stuck on 'perfection'?"

"I'm *not* stuck on…"

"Well, you're sure fooling me! What is it that you need to accomplish with *every* client before you feel 'good enough' to be a counselor?"

What the hell!

I said, "What kind of therapy do you practice?"

She said, "What kind do you need?"

Jumpin' Jehoshaphat, the woman was annoying. I didn't need to pay for therapy to get such abuse! I could get that from my *own* clients! If I had any. I had half a mind to walk out on her and leave her wondering what *she* did that was not 'good enough'.

"You are *not* what I was looking for!"

"Of course not! You wanted a mommy to hold your hand and tell you that you are a wonderful therapist and that your clients just weren't intelligent enough to appreciate what you had to offer them!"

Is *that* what I said?

"Yes, you did!"

She was reading my mind again. And I didn't like it.

"What do you think of the profession you're in?"

Huh? "What do you mean?"

She waved a hand invitingly in the air, as if she would accept any bit of self-revelation I happened to come up with. "I mean, what do you think of counseling as a profession? Do you respect it? Believe in it? Do you enjoy it? Or is it all a con game?"

"Why would you ask that?"

"Because of the way you keep coming back to that theme with what sounds like resentment."

"I sound resentful?"

"Yes, you do."

"Well, I'm not."

"Great! Then tell me how you feel about the profession you're in. Did you make a wrong career choice?"

She was wise to not follow that question up with another that would have obscured the first question and have given me a 'way out'. Did I make a wrong career choice? No, I didn't think so, but…

"…you think I'm resentful?"

"I'm just wondering, that's all. *Are* you resentful?"

When a question strikes you as hard as that one struck me, you have to pay attention to it. You have to consider the possibility.

"...I guess I do have some resentment...about some aspects of the profession."

"Such as?"

"Well...other counselors. Can we start there?"

"We can start wherever you want. What *about* other counselors?"

"Most of them are either ill-trained or parasitic. They prey on the fears of their clients. I'm appalled at the kind of 'treatment' I hear 'counselors' give their clients."

"Explain that."

"Well, the first thing they do is identify the client's problems and fears."

"Don't you do that?"

"Yes, but..."

"Yes, but, what?"

"Who's telling this? Me or you?"

"Sorry. 'They identify the client's problems.' Please continue."

"They identify the client's fears and then they feed those fears!"

"…really?…"

"Yes. They try to make the client fearful and dependent on the counselor. That keeps the client coming back. It keeps the money rolling in."

"…okay… And how does that therapy end?"

"It doesn't! That's the point! It keeps going as long as the client is willing to pay! And when the counselor can't find new ways to exacerbate the first problem, she or he 'finds another problem' that the client 'needs to think about'. I don't like that way of 'doing counseling'."

"But don't you think that all dysfunctional behaviors are connected?"

"Usually. In some way. And I believe people should have some sort of emotional support their entire lives. But that doesn't mean the counselor gets to make the decision to keep the client in therapy. That's up to the client. Not the counselor. It should be a mutually agreed upon arrangement and relationship."

"What I originally meant was, is that kind of 'therapy' successful? Would it satisfy *you* to engage your clients that way?"

"No. I wouldn't do it. I *don't* do it!"

"Do you think *all* therapists practice that way?"

"No. But some well-meaning therapists become unintentionally involved in bad therapy. They get emotionally wrapped up in their client's drama and get drawn in by their needy behavior to the point that the counselor is making decisions for them. And telling the clients how to live their lives. It may be unintentional but it *still* isn't beneficial. It produces *de*pendence not *in*dependence in the clients. And that bothers me."

"Okay. So, that's how some counselors practice. How does *that* impact you? Why does it *bother* you?"

"It cheapens the profession. It harms all of us. Counselors *and* clients."

"So, your concern is entirely altruistic?"

Okay, so she got me. "No, not entirely. It annoys me personally."

"How?"

I had to think about that one. "I hate cheaters."

"So, cheaters offend your sense of right and wrong?"

"...yeah...I guess that's right."

"So, you have a high sense of morality. Are your standards *too* high?"

"Too high for what? What's so wrong about expecting basic fairness from people? Or minimal competence from professionals?"

"Nothing. Unless your sense of fairness harms *you*."

"How could a sense of fairness harm *me*?"

"It could harm you if your standards are too high for other people to meet."

"I don't expect other people to meet my standards."

"Of course not. You only expect *you* to meet your high standards. That must be difficult to live with. Especially when nobody else is doing it."

I had to think about *that*, too. Okay, so I already *knew* about that. Maybe I just wasn't paying attention to it. "I can't be concerned with how other people choose to live."

"I agree. But maybe some of that resentment you have 'for the profession' amounts to feeling the unfairness of your situation."

Huh?

"Maybe you're not thinking about it..."

She meant it might be subconscious. Or *un*conscious.

"...but maybe the way *other* people behave is not the way *you* think people *should* behave. Does that sound about right?"

She was inching me toward something. Exchange by exchange, she was pushing me toward…what? An emotional cliff? Did she expect me to fly, don Juan? "I guess so."

"Was that how you were raised? Or did you come to that conclusion on your own?"

"A bit of both, I guess."

"And, how's that working for you?"

Cute. Is that how *I* sounded to *my* clients when *I* said things like that? "So, are you suggesting that my standards are too high and that I should lighten up and become as corrupt as everyone else?"

"You're too experienced not to notice that there is a *wee* bit of anger in that question. Who are you mad at?"

Damn! She knew darn well who I was mad at.

"So, when are you going to stop punishing yourself?"

"Punishing myself for what?"

"Maybe that's what you came here to find out."

"Well, then, help me find it out!" Okay, so I was angry.

"Okay." Bless her little heart, she didn't challenge my anger - which was so obviously present. She gave me an emotional breather. Or maybe she was just collecting ammunition for her next barrage. "So, you don't like unethical therapists. What else don't you like about the profession you've chosen?"

"Notes."

We both laughed. Keeping files was a sort of 'necessary evil.' It was required by law but not always the most pleasant chore to keep up with.

"What don't you like about keeping notes?"

"There's no point to it!"

"What do you mean?"

"I never *read* the things! I remember all the pertinent information about my clients, so what's the point of keeping files that most of the time *no*body ever reads?"

She just 'gave me a look', so I explained.

"I grew up knowing all about Richard Nixon and Lewis Fielding. I've never had any illusions about the sanctity of a counselor's private files."

"Lewis Fielding? Don't you mean Daniel Ellsberg?"

Once again, we were sparring with one another in a kind of intellectual one-ups-man-ship. It was snobby of both of us but we knew we understood each other. (Google it! Then you can be snooty, too.)

"They were Fielding's notes!"

She nodded. "Point taken. What about it?"

"Before that time, clients had the notion that anything they said in a counseling session was privileged information. The counselor couldn't reveal it and the courts couldn't demand it. But after Ellsberg's personal information was splattered all over the front page of the *New York Times*, lawyers declared open season on confidential files."

"That *was* annoying for the profession."

"Before Ellsberg, *some* counselors thought that files should consist of personal notes *from* the therapist *to* the therapist to *remind* the therapist of where he and the client were in the work they were doing. The notes included objective information about what the client talked about as well as subjective reports on how the client behaved and responded in the session. They also contained the thoughts, feelings and impressions of the therapist to help her or him stay focused on the goals of the therapy. Files were never meant to be read by anyone other than the counselor who *wrote* them. Not even the client was supposed to be able to see them because it was thought that the counselor's private reflections might harm the client's progress."

"Yes. And...?"

"After Ellsberg, lawyers discovered they could breach the privilege of the client and the confidentiality required of the therapist and get their eyes on anything they wanted. That changed the way counselors kept their files. It's one thing to write personal, private, confidential notes to yourself and another thing to write for worldwide publication in the tabloids. Think about it! If you thought there might be a scandal in there somewhere – or a movie deal - wouldn't you compose your notes in a more circumspect manner? Focus them in one direction or another?"

"How did this concern affect *your* note keeping?"

"It's a funny thing about that. At first I wrote notes to protect my clients. I never put anything down on paper that could potentially harm them. If a guy told me he just beat his wife within an inch of her life, I would write 'client discussed recent marital conflict.' If a woman disclosed a five year affair with her husband's best friend, I would write, 'client mentioned some dissatisfaction with her partner's lovemaking.' That way if I were ever pulled into court, I could be as vague as my notes and if necessary I could claim that I didn't remember exactly what the note referred to. Then the lawyers could argue that they thought I was incompetent, but they couldn't use the files *against* anyone. I thought I was *protecting* my clients! And I guess that would have protected everybody but the problem was that the files became useless to *me*! If I couldn't keep an honest record of what we were working on and what I was thinking, that file did me no good! It wasn't written as a tool to focus and further the work, it was written merely to meet the requirements of the law and circumvent the intrusions of the lawyers!"

"And somehow you changed your mind?"

"Yeah, actually. I did."

"How did that come about?"

"Well, I learned through practical experience that the *only* people who wanted to read my files were my clients, themselves, or my clients' lawyers! It was the *clients* who invoked their 'right' to see my files on them and forced me to turn them over! I thought that counseling files were supposed to be personal notes *from* myself *to* myself. But the *clients* insisted they had a *right* to know what I was *think*ing about them! My *clients* became my *thought* police! Big Brother, move over!"

"What did that do to your note keeping?"

"It changed my perspective one hundred and eighty degrees. Instead of *protecting* my clients, I wrote only things that would *harm* them! I recorded all of their personal information, their secrets and their crimes, their affairs, fetishes and perversions! Mind you, that didn't make the files any more useful to *me*. As treatment tools they were still worthless. But if a client ever dragged a file into court, it could be potentially harmful or embarrassing to the client but it was less likely to hurt *me*. That didn't help the client but it could protect me."

"Sounds like you were at war with your clients."

"That was not how I wanted it to be. It's just how it worked out."

"So how did you resolve the conflict?"

"Simple. I stopped writing notes."

"...stopped writing notes..."

"Yeah."

"And what will you do if someone demands to see their file?"

"I've got that covered."

"I see."

I paused. She paused. It was a 'who blinks first' kind of a challenge but she was professional enough to decline the gambit.

"We seem to be getting closer to the stressors that brought you here. Are there any others that you can identify?"

"Oh, a lifetime of personal conflicts, I guess. Like anybody else. And, like you mentioned, I seem to have isolated myself lately. No social life to speak of. I just don't seem to be interested in anything anymore. But don't worry," I said, flashing a mischievous look into her eyes in order to head off any concern she might legally and ethically be forced to pursue, "I'm not going to harm myself."

"That's good to know," she said. "Saves us all that pointless recitation of Tarasoff."

I smiled. She didn't. The Tarasoff decision is the counseling profession's version of Miranda Rights: it requires a counselor to assess a client's potential to harm self or others and to take action to prevent such harm. I knew she was in the process of that very assessing. If I worried her enough, she would have to call in the goon squad. I stopped smiling. "I'm fine," I assured her. "I promise."

"Okay. So, you're fine. Can we say that you're experiencing…some depression?"

"…yeah…some…"

"Induced by…work related stress?"

"…I guess that's accurate enough…"

"Any other stressors? Marital?"

"I'm not married. You know that."

"Things change. I had to ask. Personal relationship troubles?"

"No relationship at the moment."

"Family of origin conflicts? Aging parents? Sibling strife?"

I shook my head. I knew she had to work her way through the check list. "No, none of those."

"Financial issues? Income problems?"

"I have enough money to pay your fee, if you're worried about that."

"Doug, I wasn't worried about my fee. I would be happy and honored to consult with you at any time as a professional courtesy."

I was touched by her generosity but there was no way I could let that show. "You're not going to make your fortune doing pro bono work."

"How about you?" she said. "Do much pro bono work of your own, do you?"

From the way she asked that question, I knew that she must have known about my 'pro bono work'. I chose not to respond, so she picked up the thread of the previous conversation.

"You haven't answered. How *are* your finances? Any stressors concerning money?"

"Yeah, well... I'm getting down to the wire there. That's probably one of the reasons I called."

"How can I help you with that?"

"...I've got to make a decision...pretty soon, I think..."

"A decision about what?"

"...uuhhh...a career decision. I've got to decide what I do next."

She paused; reflected, I thought. "What are you thinking about doing? Changing your specialty? Re-opening your office? ...or changing your line of work...?"

"...uuhh... I've been toying with the latter."

"I see." She took a few beats. "That would be a loss to the community."

"I don't think 'the community' would notice."

"I do. What are you thinking about going into?"

"I don't know, really. I've always wanted to chuck it all and go crew on a sailing ship. Something small, you know, that couples could rent for a week at a time to go on vacation. Only a captain and me – sort of like Gilligan but with sails. A schooner, a sloop or a bark. Maybe a Sampan. Anything that floats that I could get hired on. If I was the crew I wouldn't have to worry about expenses, budgets, bills or anything. No stress. No worries. Just the sun and the undulating ocean. That'd be nice."

"A *Bark*?"

I noticed she passed on my suggestion of 'Sampan.' Maybe she knew the idea was more whimsical than practical.

"Wouldn't a sloop be too small to require a crew?"

I shrugged.

"So, you'd like to run away from your troubles and lose yourself on…what? The high seas? The *undulating* ocean?"

I smiled. It did sound funny when you said it like that.

"I've got to tell you, the cannon don't thunder, there ain't nothin' to plunder and you're a bit old to start goin' bare foot out on the yardarms."

"Do you kill everyone's dreams?"

"No," she said. "No, I don't. I like to support them. When I can. But disappearing into the South Pacific isn't your real dream. What you're really saying is that you'd like to escape. What do you want to escape *from*? What's hurting you?"

"I'd have to think about that."

"Well, while you're thinking, tell me something. Have you been seeing clients lately?"

"Yes…sort of."

"What kind of cases have you been working on?"

"Oh, you know. The same old this and that. General issues. Relationship conflicts. Employment dissatisfaction. Anxiety. Depression. Incest. Abortion. Drug addiction. Self-mutilation. Degradation. Hopelessness. Despair."

We both laughed. Gallows humor: sad but true.

"And what does it cost you to do that work?"

"What does it *cost* me? What do you mean?"

"How much of yourself do you have to surrender in order to sit with those general issues, relationship conflicts, employment dissatisfactions, anxiety, depression, incest, abortions, drug addictions, self-mutilations, degradations, hopelessness and despair?"

It seemed I wasn't the *only* counselor with the trick of remembering what clients said. "I'm still not getting you."

"Doug, from what I can see, you seem to invest a lot of your personal and emotional energy in your work and in your clients. Is that part of the counseling technique that you use?"

"What do you mean? I'm not supposed to *care* about my clients?"

"You can care about your clients but if that caring has a harmful effect on you, if it drains you of your ability to empathize, won't it eventually make you incapable of *do*ing the work?"

"I don't think it's draining me of my ability to empathize."

"It's not? Then tell me – honestly – how do you feel about your clients?"

"You already asked me that."

"Yes, I did. And since we're further along in our conversation and you've had some time to reflect on all the issues we've been talking about, I'm asking again. With the hope that you might actually answer this time."

"What do you mean, how do I *feel* about my clients? People are interesting. Human behavior is fascinating! *I think my clients are interesting!*"

"But that's not a feeling. Are you in love with your clients?"

"No! The people who come to me are usually not loveable. At least not at the start."

"Okay, then. Do you hate them?"

"Not that, either. I just find them... *interesting*. Uniquely interesting. Like waves on the ocean, no two people are exactly alike."

"Okay. So you don't love them and you don't hate them. You have no feeling about them at all. You're numb!"

"Yeah...something like that."

"Okay. Then what do you get out of it?"

"Besides money?"

"Besides money. What do you get out of doing this work?"

"...uh... Satisfaction. Mental and professional stimulation. A sense of purpose...and meaning in life."

"Do all your clients give you satisfaction, purpose and meaning?"

"No. Of course not."

"How many, then? Percentage wise, what per cent of your clients give you satisfaction?"

"...well, uh... Lately, that would be kind of low."

"How would you say you feel about the majority of your clients…lately?"

"…aahbbuh…"

"Come on, tell me. How do you feel about your clients *lately*?"

"…I don't know…"

"How much do they pay you?"

"Isn't that a rather *personal* question? I mean, clients come on a sliding scale. I don't think that…"

"Let me put it another way. Why don't you collect fees?"

"Who ever said a thing like that? I collect fees."

"Like what? Eggs, chickens, goats? Milk? Wash your car? Wax your surfboard? The word is all over the beach about what you're doing. Why don't you collect fees?"

"…I, uh… Well… The thing is…"

"Are you *mad* at your clients? You said earlier that you *resent* them."

"I didn't actually *mean* that. Why would I resent my clients?"

"For what they've taken away from you."

"What have they..."

"Your satisfaction, purpose and meaning. Your dignity as a counselor. Your self-worth. Are you mad at your clients? Or just mad at the world?"

"Look, I'm not..."

"Want me to tell you what *I'm* guessing is the reason you won't accept fees?"

"No, not really. My choice of..."

"As a result of this conversation I'm guessing that you won't accept fees because you think that *that* will protect you from your clients and their lawyers."

"*That's* an interesting idea! How do you..."

"You think that if no compensation is received, it's not a professional contract and therefore you can't be held liable if a client is dissatisfied. And – coincidently – if it's *not* professional counseling, you *don't* have to write notes! Which protects you on the issue of keeping files. Is that about what you're thinking?"

"Well, I couldn't say that, uh... But I'll give it some thought. Thanks for the idea of..."

"Doug, when are you going to tell me about the law suit?"

"The *law* suit? What has *that* got to do with...?"

"Is *that* why you decided to drop out of the human race? To escape by sailing the seven seas? To act out your contempt and anger by *not* accepting fees? I mean, if your *clients* don't think you're worth anything, the hell with them! *You* don't need their money! You don't need *them*! Is *that* why you're here?"

"Well, look. I'll admit that some of my personal feelings have been affecting my work but, uhm..."

"Affecting your work? Doug, you've let all this de*stroy* you! Have you ever heard of 'professional distance'? You can empathize with your clients – you can sincerely *care* about them -

but you can't take their pain home with you! You have to leave it at the door. You have to drop it off somewhere, somehow! At the end of your pier – I don't care! You give too much of yourself. You wear your heart on your sleeve. What good can you do yourself or anyone else if you sacrifice your life to be a sin eater? No one can hold as much pain as counselors are asked to on a daily basis! No one who cares and wants to be of service! Where do you drop it off? How do you get rid of it? You're taking care of everybody else! How do you take care of your*self*?"

Silence.

Then more silence.

She wasn't going to let me off the hook by speaking another word. She wanted an answer.

"…I walk the pier…"

"…I know… I've been watching. We've all been watching. All your friends in the profession. And we've been hoping you would drop in on one of us."

"And you lost."

"No. …I won. Doug, tell me about the law suit."

"What's to tell? A client got mad. I got sued. End of story."

"Begin at the beginning. Tell me every detail. Every feeling you had long the way. Tell it all."

"I don't know… That way it could be a long story. Isn't the hour over?"

"I've cleared my schedule. I'm here for as long as this takes."

"That long, huh. What is this? 'Encounter' therapy? When is this session going to end?"

"*End*? *I'm* wondering when it's going to *start*."

"So, this is an open-ended endurance marathon meant to wear me down?"

"Never mind what it is."

"When do I get to stop?"

"You'll know. We'll both know. Right now the important thing is to *begin*."

"There's really not much to tell. I asked a simple, standard, counselor-type question and it upset the client."

"What did you ask?"

"I asked her what she did to contribute to her conflict with her family - how she participated in her problems with her relatives - and she went berserk. She insisted that she hadn't done anything then she started yelling. And then she went home, screamed at her mother, the relatives complained, they all sued and the rest was history."

"Start from the beginning. Tell me all the details. How long had you been seeing the client? What were the issues you were working on?"

"I had been working with that client about three months. Every session she wanted to complain about her mother and her sister. She said her father and her brother just stayed out of the 'family feud' as she called it."

"What was the family feuding about?"

"Everything. Basically it was a fused, enmeshed family system. Each member was dysfunctionally involved in the lives of the others. The sister was married, the client was divorced and the three women argued about every aspect of each others' lives."

"Such as?"

"The client said her mother and sister blamed her for getting divorced, even though the client blamed her ex-husband for all the problems in their relationship. The client said the husband drank too much and never came home. She suspected he was having affairs but she had no proof of it. When the husband asked for a divorce, she said 'Great! Let's *end* this travesty of a marriage!' Her family thought she should have tried to work it out. The client thought the *sister's* marriage was a mess that needed a divorce and said so. The mother told the sisters to have a drink and love each other – in that order. Sister called mother an alcoholic. Mother took umbrage and triangulated with the client who didn't appreciate mother hanging out in her condo drinking while client was at work.

"Client eventually threw mother out of her condo. Mother went back to triangulate with the sister and those two decided that the client should 'just get over it' and go hook another 'poor sap' – client's words – before she was 'too ragged out for any bastard to want her' – sister's prognosis. Client took offense and told them to 'go to hell' which was when the two harpies – client's description – ganged up and *really* went after her. The harpies – client's appellation – berated client's dress, her walk, her talk, her hair style, even the way she breathed. Client had narcoleptic sleep apnea which caused her to 'nod out' and snort during the harpies' – my use of the client's choice of appellation – harangues of her. Client's feelings were hurt. She wanted to isolate but just couldn't bring herself to leave her loving family. So one day client stormed over to mother's house to confront sister and ran afoul of her brother who became disgusted with the father for not putting a stop to all of the 'bull shit' - brother's description. Brother told father he wasn't a man and had never been a good role model for the son's son so the son wasn't going to belittle himself by bringing *his* family to the grandparents' 'lunatic asylum' any more.

"Son went home – told all this to his wife. Wife came back to engage in the battle because she felt she had been left out of all the fun. Horrible things were said on all sides. Papa showed that he was truly the patriarch of the loony bin by pouring brandy in mother's coffee cup. Mother denounced father for his loutishness in not knowing that brandy was an 'after dinner aperitif' – her misunderstanding, not mine - and mixed cocktails for the lot of them. Sister got drunk and slobbered an apology all over the client. Wife got in her cups and demanded an apology, too. With a smirk, father slipped out of the house. *His* work was done! Mother swallowed a whiskey sour right out of the bottle just to catch up and – hugging sister and wife - declared that that's why God created families. That's when the client just got drunk."

"…yes…and…?"

"Client came to see me and wanted to know why she was depressed."

"How did any of *that* end up involving *you* in a law suit?"

"I attempted to assist the client in sorting out the issues. We talked about assertiveness and setting boundaries – in that particular case, in not allowing her family members to draw her into their conflicts. I suggested she stop drinking – especially with her family – and start attending Alcoholics Anonymous and/or Adult Children of Alcoholics meetings. She said she stopped drinking – I don't believe she did – and that she had begun insisting that her relatives leave her out of their squabbles. During one session, she told me she felt real proud of herself because she had finally stood up to them by telling 'em all to 'stuff it up their bung holes.' I told her that wasn't exactly the idea we were going for. We were looking for peace and resolution, not more conflict."

"What did she say to that?"

"She sort of didn't say anything. She got quiet and I was concerned that she was withdrawing from me. I didn't want her to isolate. I wanted her to *talk*. She promised she would be back for the next session."

"Did she come back?"

"Yes, she did. And she told me an interesting story. She said the intervening weekend she went to her parents' house in order to 'have it out once and for all.' She was going to be a 'grown woman' and they weren't going to stop her!"

"Not what you were going for."

"No. Not *at all* what *I* was going for! But it seemed to fit the client's agenda perfectly!

"Anyway…client went to her parents' house and demanded that they treat her like a woman. Papa said, 'Fine! Of course! That's all we ever wanted!' and mixed her a highball. After the two of them shared their second father and daughter peace-making libation, papa said, 'Let's be done with our differences once and for all! Let's get 'em all out, deal with 'em and then forget them forever! Okay?' Client said, okay, that's fine. A good idea. So papa puts his hands on client's shoulders, looks her in the eye and says, 'Daughter, I love you. I really do.' He kisses her – on the mouth – sexually. Shoves his tongue half-way down her esophagus. Then he hauls off and slaps her - violently – openhanded, across the face. Almost knocks the drunken client unconscious. When client regains what was left of her senses, papa says, 'All right, then! I got it off my chest! I feel great. Thank you!' Client can't believe what has just happened. Then papa says, 'Now, you! Go ahead. Get it out! It'll make you feel better.' Client doesn't want any part of it. Especially the kissing.

"Mama comes in – finds papa pawing her daughter - the client - and insisting on an 'I love you' kiss that was supposed to make all their differences go away. Also finds client fuming at papa. Mama asks what's going on. As papa is telling the story – and client is rebutting every word of it – mama mixes the luncheon Martini. Papa talks, mama downs the first half-liter. Client talks, mama downs the second. Papa starts to defend himself and mama decides that *she* is the one to settle the family feud. While mama is educating both of them on how to live their lives, sister comes in with her husband and *they* mix connubial cocktails. Mama tells the story of the events of the afternoon – which she never saw – sister pours, husbands drinks. Brother comes in and wants to know what's going on. So husband pours, brother drinks and sister tells the story of the events of the afternoon that she heard from mother who wasn't there and didn't see any of it.

"Client screams, 'Enough of this shit! You're all making me crazy!' and makes herself a 'Golden Grasshopper'. That's a drink the client created that she said helped her forget who she was related to. Basically, you just pour every kind of alcohol into a large glass.

"Anyway…

"After listening to – and correcting – the story that she has now heard – and told - several times but never actually witnessed, mother decides that papa had the right idea in the first place. 'Let's all kiss and make up!' So, mama finishes her latest Gimlet, sets down her glass and goes over to her son-in-law, the client's sister's husband – seizes him by the neck and shoulders, kisses him full opened-mouth, steps back and bashes him with a bone-shattering, closed fisted, right cross to the chin. Then mama shouts, 'Now, *you* do it! Get it out! Make you feel good! Then we'll *all* be done with it and *this* family will be *normal* for a change!' Next, mama decides to continue the family normalization process by attempting to French-kiss her daughter, the client.

"Dumbfounded – and fearing an ensuing round-house kick to the groin - client pushes mother away screaming, 'You're crazy! You're *all* fuckin' crazy!' Sister doesn't appreciate client's use of profanity and steps up to tell her so. But sister's so drunk, she can't get the words out. So sister shakes client in an attempt to induce dislocation of the fourth cervical vertebrae – which sister expects will somehow help client understand her umbrage of the profanity. Client pushes sister off of her. Husband – who always said he never liked client in the first place – grabs client and tells her 'Don't ever put hands on my wife!' Then husband kisses client violently on the mouth.

"Brother pulls husband off of client and shouts, 'You're drunk! Leave her to me!' Sister slaps brother. Mother shouts, 'Don't fight! If you have to slap someone, slap me!' Client slaps mother. Father laughs hysterically. Mother slaps father. Father grabs client and says, '*You're* responsible for all of this shit!' and pushes client. Client stumbles backward and falls through the sliding glass patio door. Everybody's shouting and screaming. Neighbors call the cops. Police show up and arrest the client for assault and battery, mutual combat, terrorist threats, drunk and disorderly, disturbing the peace, destruction of personal property and assorted misdemeanors."

"So, how did all that involve you?"

"When the thing appeared in court, mother sided with her husband and blamed my client. Sister, her husband and brother went along for the ride and blamed my client. My client blamed *me*. Said *I* was the one who told her to do everything she did. Family's lawyers sued me and demanded that I produce my records of the client's counseling. Through *my* lawyers, I cited client confidentiality and privilege and refused to present the file in court because *I* thought it would harm my client. Judge locked me up for contempt of court, client sued me for 'breach of contract' and the local constabulary broke into my office and confiscated the client's file.

"At that time I was still writing session notes in a style to protect my client even though that made the file worthless to me as a therapeutic tool. My very expensive lawyers told me I had nothing to worry about and that I wouldn't be found guilty of any wrong-doing. But my professional insurance company decided it would be cheaper to settle the matter out of court than to go through the trial.

"So my professional insurance company gave my client and her family several hundred thousand dollars, the family dropped their allegations against me and the court eventually dismissed the entire mess. But by then, my client-protecting notes – the ones that minimized the client's dysfunctional behavior - had been published in part on the front pages of the local newspapers and I was made to look incompetent and unethical. My insurance company cancelled my insurance – not for the lawsuit but for the alleged incompetence and public ridicule - which meant I couldn't get any more professional insurance so I had to stop conducting therapy as an individual practitioner. The *other* clients that I had at the time all quietly drifted away during the court proceedings and I…"

"...you, what...?"

"...I didn't want to do counseling anymore."

"You felt betrayed. By a client you tried to help. If I may ask, how much was your session fee for that client?"

"Why would you ask that?"

"Just a hunch. How much?"

"...well... She was recently divorced and trying to re-establish herself financially. She had made a large down payment on her condo. She felt alone, hopeless..."

"How much?"

"...I used a sliding scale... I was going to re-coup when her situation stabilized."

"So, you were seeing her for bupkiss and she knifed you in your accounts receivable. Doesn't seem fair, does it?"

"I'm not a victim in all this. I knew what I was doing. I made a decision and I will live with the consequences."

"No, you're not a victim. That kind of self-indulgence is for clients. You're the solid, stable, rescuer type who sacrifices everything he has for the good of mankind and the Ya-Ya Sisterhood. Why do you do that? Did your mother invalidate your experiences? Deny your feelings? Do you need validation that you didn't get from your family or your personal relationships? You already know this stuff, but identify for me the transactional behavior patterns in your family of origin. Did your family support you? Encourage you? Or was there an emotional cut-off somewhere along the way? A non-recognition of your talents, successes and abilities or did they tell you that you didn't *deserve* any of them? Is that why you 'do not choose' to accept fees? Are you self-abnegating? Self-immolating? Self-defeating? Are your feelings of unworthiness that were engendered in childhood exacerbating your feelings about the lawsuit and that client? After all that, I can't help but wonder if maybe you give away a *little* too much of yourself. But, that's just me, I guess."

"What the heck does *that* mean? Are we supposed to kill off our feelings?"

"No. But ethically we have to not involve ourselves with our clients to the point that it harms us. We can't help anybody else if we fall apart, ourselves. I mean, look at your situation. You tried to help somebody – for little or no fee – and she blamed you for all her problems and *sued* you for choices *she* made. Ultimately she hurt you professionally and financially and she walked away without making any substantive improvement in her behavior *or* her life. *You* were betrayed and penalized…that must have left you with *some* resentment. You almost wouldn't be human if it didn't."

"She was a *client*! We can't blame clients for being clients! That's why they come to us!"

"Yes. And we owe them professional care. But we don't owe them our *lives*. We don't owe them our *careers*. And we certainly don't owe them our *licenses* - which we worked long and hard to get! What we *owe* them is every bit of professionalism we can provide, *nothing* more."

"I *did* all that!"

"Yeah! And then you went on a self-pity binge to prove to the world that you're a viable candidate for a 5150 mental status evaluation! Where are your sack cloth and ashes? Out there at the end of your pier? On the fo'c'sle of your Sampan?"

"A Sampan doesn't have a fo'c'sle. I don't think. What are you trying to say?"

"I'm saying you've been reacting emotionally and not professionally. From all the stories you've told me, it appears you've forgotten all your counseling skills and your appropriate emotional distance in your work. You've given into your negative feelings, anger and resentment."

"I've tried to be a good therapist."

"Good therapist! All you've done is re-enact a narcissistic wound. That's not therapy! That's self-abuse! You were a solid counselor at one time and respected on the beach. You *know* that good therapy doesn't consist of 'a bag of counseling tricks'. Therapy is a *relationship* that takes time to establish and a *trust* that takes time to earn. Only *then* can you explore a client's deeper beliefs and faulty behavior."

"I don't use 'tricks'. I use proven counseling technique."

"Yeah, well, your 'technique' sucks. Did you bother to make a therapeutic alliance with that Austin's client? Or did you just bash her around with your acting out? Do you set any goals? Do you even *try* to connect with your clients? Or do you just attack them with 'Phase Two Interpretations' during the first meeting? That doesn't have substance, insight, interaction *or* understanding and it's of *no* value to any client. Everything you've told me is crap! It's just your ego manifesting and acting out your resentment. It's *crap* psychology."

"And *this* is crap, too. Where is *your* empathy?"

"I'm sitting here listening to all your self-pity, aren't I? That's empathy enough for one day. You need to complete your *own* therapy before you pretend to therapize anybody else."

"I thought that's why I came to you. Why are you so mad at me?"

"I'm mad because you have pissed me off! You've demolished every therapeutic requirement known to the profession. And the thing that makes me crazy is that you *know* all this! You're deliberately sabotaging your career and your life out of some petulance you think is self-righteousness."

"Don't I have a right to *some* feelings?"

"Of course you do. But your self-destruction doesn't give you a right to shove a client in a direction she's not ready to go. Phase Two Interpretation, my ass! A client's resistance is a signal to the therapist that the *client* isn't getting what she needs to move on in the therapy process. You were pushing the client in the *wrong* direction!"

"Like *you* are pushing *me* right now. I thought you just said that that was poor technique for a therapist."

"I'm not your therapist and I'm not *going* to be your therapist. I'm your friend. We'll *get* you an appropriate counselor. But right now, what I want is - I want to see you walk back in off the plank - pull yourself out of this depression you're in. Have you been attending to your own needs? Have you been seeing to your own self-care? No! That's why I'm mad at you! You know as well as everybody else in this business what you need to do to protect your emotional well-being and you're *not* doing it!"

"Well, I was just trying to help my client. She *needed* help. Probably still does."

"What? Are you saying that if that client who sued you came to you today, you would resume working with her?"

"Yes, I would. I believe in the philosophy of 'once a client, always a client.' It's a way to maintain the relationship and to solidify the work that was done."

"Oh, my lord... By that token, everybody you ever meet is a client. Doesn't that leave you rather isolated?"

"I get by."

"My gosh! So if that 'client from hell' returned and you continued to work with her, what would you hope to accomplish?"

"Connection. Trust. Understanding. That's what *you* said she needed in the first place and hasn't received."

"But *you*'re not in a position to provide those things. She *sued* you!"

"I'm aware of what she did."

"Then, why..."

"Maybe she's learned something from the experience! Maybe she's figured out what went wrong. The woman was emotionally drowned in her dysfunctional, alcoholic family. Maybe she's realized it and wants to begin some honest work on discovering herself!"

"In a pig's eye! Families that enmeshed don't change until the universe collapses on them – which never happens. And all the lawyers and your insurance company did was to co-dependently support them in their insanity. They rewarded them! Right now, those people are out having a party! They aren't thinking about 'honest work to discover themselves'."

"Aaah, maybe so. But if she came to me and asked for help, I would provide it. That's what I signed on for. Wouldn't *you* if she came *here* and asked *you* for help?"

"Probably not! No counselor in her right mind would work with a client who's looking for a free-lunch ticket from an insurance company! But if for some reason I *had* to agree to work with her, I'd force her to sign an absolute, iron-clad, no-fault, bonded, non-litigation agreement before I'd let her into the building!"

"I don't know. I'll bet if she were here, you would work with her."

"But right now, she's *not* here! *She's* not my client! *You* are my client and I'm looking out for *your* best interests, not *hers*!"

"A minute ago you told me you were my *friend*, not my therapist."

"Whatever. I reserve a friend's right to be whatever you need."

She shook her head and said, "Doug, you've got to maintain some professional distance in this business. I suspect your entire social life is talking to clients. You've become too involved with them! You're like a walking Stockholm Syndrome."

"She's not a bank robber and I'm not identifying with her."

"Are you sure? How much counseling or peer supervision have you had since the trial? How many consultations? How much have you looked into your synchronic issues? I'm not asking you to vilify your clients! I'm asking you to look at your own part in the life you're created for yourself *after* you experienced *that particular* client. Where else does your recent self-destruction come from? *Why* are you doing it?"

"I refuse to answer on the grounds that it may tend to incriminate me."

"Yeah! And where do you go from there? After you refuse to incriminate yourself and run off the end of the tectonic plate, what next? Escape to the South Seas in a *Bark*? Go off for some Adventures in Paradise? As a foremast jack? And when some rich bastard falsely accuses you of winking at his mistress who's lying naked on the poop deck, are you going to take the 'Patusan' up river, Lord Jim? When do you stop running? Where do you make a stand to take care of your*self*?"

"A bark doesn't have a poop deck. Lord Jim's ship was the 'Patna'. 'Patusan' was a settlement, not a ship. It was an ocean, not a river. That was Heart of Darkness, I think. And I'm not running. I've never left the beach area. I'm right here – at the scene of the crime."

"Not exactly. This is *my* office. When was the last time you were in *your* office?"

"Did you want me to answer that?"

"Yes! Now, that I think of it. Yes! When was the last time you were in your *own* office? When was the last time you *actually* saw a client on a professional, paying basis *in your own office?*"

"I see clients all the time."

"Yeah, for no fees. What is *that* all about? Is it some penance for your sins? Your Original Sin? Of having been born? Or are you just acting out your anger like a petulant adolescent? *Did* your mother invalidate your experiences? Deny your feelings? Or did that *girl*friend mess you up? A love affair gone south of the line? Do you need validation that you don't get anywhere else in your life? Do you need your clients to *love* you? *Admire* you? Is that why you don't accept fees?"

"What I charge is my business. Besides, how do you know what my fees are?"

"Oh, please! It's all over the beach! 'Some crazy therapist is giving away free counseling services in exchange for stupid human tricks!' In the counseling business, *you're* the talk of the town!"

"Well, I'm glad I amuse all of you."

"We're not amused. We're worried. How are you living? How are you paying your bills?"

"I had some money saved up."

"Yeah, great. Have you run out yet?"

"Almost."

"Wonderful. And what's the plan now? Assuming that Captain Ahab doesn't send for you?"

"I don't know. I haven't thought about it."

"Yeah, well, while you're submitting applications to Kon Tiki, consider this. You are wasting your talents, your empathy, your education and your life!"

"People change their occupations all the time. They decide they've had enough of one career and try something different. Something new."

"Yeah, but when they do, the transition usually makes sense. They explore the changes they're thinking about. They talk to people. They prepare. They make a plan. What's *your* plan?"

"I'm getting there."

"Really? Well, before you sail off to stand twenty years before the mast, let me make a suggestion. Ask yourself *one* question. When you've answered that, you can go be Captain Maturin if you want. None of us will care."

"It was two years."

"Huh?"

"The book Richard Henry Dana Jr. wrote was entitled *Two* Years Before The Mast. And in Patrick O'Brian's series of novels about the nineteenth century British Navy, the captain was Jack Aubrey. *Doctor* Steven Maturin was the…"

"*Whatever*! It just goes to show what you're thinking about these days! Escape! As far as the books go, nobody cares!"

"Gee, thanks. What's the question?"

"The question is this: who are you mad at? Who are you *really* mad at? When you know the answer to that, you'll be free to go and do whatever you want."

"Well, now, thanks, doctor. Wonderful session. What do I owe you?"

"I'm glad you asked. Let's do what a friend of mine does. A very *good* friend, a talented guy who thinks more of his clients and his work than he thinks of himself. A professional man with many great qualities but he doesn't honor them. A man who..."

"All right. All right. What is it?"

"Let's let the punishment fit the crime. Your payment is in two parts. First, you've got to answer the question I just asked you: Who are you mad at? This is an honor system thing. You've got to do it because you *promised* you would do it."

"I did?"

"You will if you want to get out of here!"

"Well, in *that* case, I promise. What's the second part?"

"The second part is, you have to go *back* to your office and read the files of all the clients you have worked with. Every word in every file – whether the notes mean anything to you or not – then you've got to come back here and convince me that you've read them. Do you agree to my fees?"

"That's three things."

"Whatever. Do you agree?"

"Why do you want me to read all my files?"

"I want you to remember what it's like to be a therapist. I want you to remember how to *be* the therapist that you *are*."

"…hmm… So, those are your demands for payment? If I answer your question, read my files and report back to you, we're squared? We're even?"

"Yep!"

"And if I don't agree?"

"Then you'll owe me into eternity."

"What if I agree to your fee and don't pay it?"

"If you don't pay, I'll tell everybody – all the other counselors in the beach area – and we'll all let you lie in your wounds."

Beat.

"Can I think about it?"

"Think all you want. But you *know* how to do this. You have until Tuesday to get back here with my fees."

"Tuesday? Why Tuesday?"

"Why not? It's as arbitrary as anything *you* ask *your* clients to do!"

I left thinking it was a contract made in hell.

It was.

***

I didn't immediately go back to my office. The office I hadn't entered in the previous eighteen months. That would have been unthinkable. And thinking was what I needed to do.

I returned to my pier – my anchor in good times and in bad. And I walked – each step a tradition and a ritual. In that moment – a ritual of healing.

Self-care? She accused me of neglecting self-care?

I took a step and felt the planks reverberate under my feet. What could be more self-caring than the echoes of a lifetime? The stability of a faithful friend?

The thronging crowd was accommodating that day and seemed to give way as I passed. Maybe they could see what I couldn't see: a dead man walking. A ghost. An emotional shell. That's another thing I have always appreciated about the regular visitors to the Old Town Pier: like the gentle Pacific, they knew when to part and to allow someone his serenity.

I walked a well-beaten path – the one beaten by me – and knew that I had arrived at a tidal shift. Decisions had to be made. Plans had to be formulated. Yet I was in no condition to make the one or to formulate the other.

I only knew the pier – the walk – would give me answers.

***

Whenever I have shared stories of my counseling experiences, I think the important part is the journey to self-discovery. How did we get to where we were and what did we learn? What did we do with that new-found knowledge and where would we go from there? For me, those are the significant parts. But audiences of one or a hundred or a thousand want to know how the story ends. How it turned out. I was still working on that part of my story. I knew it would take a while and I wanted to get it right.

But I thought there was time enough for that.

After all, I had until Tuesday.

Wounded Healer

*

And whatever happened to that Wounded Healer? The physician who went out during a great conflict to tend to his brothers who were lying injured?

Wasn't it obvious?

Eventually he succumbed to his wounds.

And died on the field of battle.

Finis

*

Bonus Section: from
<u>Shamarla</u>

The third dumpster gave me pause. Perhaps my native superstitions had just kicked in. Or perhaps there was some truth to the notion of 'third on a match' and 'the third time's the charm.' I didn't know. But I was certain I didn't want to raise that lid. I stood frozen before that hulking metal chamber and somehow knew that my life was about to change. I was reconsidering my options when I heard an almost silent whimper - like the gasp of a soul that didn't want to leave being sucked into the afterlife. It wasn't the loud and full of terror wail of a tormented sinner recoiling from his just desserts. No, rather it was a soft, plaintive gasp, the melancholy sigh of a soul who had only glimpsed the circus that she would never be allowed to enjoy.

I had the notion that what I heard was the last breath of an innocent who no longer had the strength to protest.

Damn the rats, I thought as I threw open the lid.

My impressions had not been wrong. Before my eyes that were adjusting to the shadows in the dumpster lay a baby nestled in a cardboard box. A box that had been settled on top of the other debris in such a way that suggested care, concern and a type of lamenting love for what could not be. At first I didn't want to touch it, for fear that I had been called there to witness the infant's passing – her crossing over. But finally I dropped my pepper spray into my coat pocket, drove my hands around the baby and scooped her out of her cardboard coffin. As I held her up before my eyes, I could see that she was a newborn, her face barely unwrinkled from her amniotic seclusion. I could feel that she was virtually weightless – more of a possibility, a suggestion; more spirit than person. And cold, so very cold. The rags she wore would never have been enough to keep out the icy fingers of death. And she was beautiful. A porcelain goddess too perfect for this life. Too perfect, too fragile, too ethereal to survive on this cruel human plane.

As I stared into her motionless face, too overcome to give into my growing shock or to the tears that were piling up around my eyes – tears that had gathered without permission - I had the uncontrollable urge to place my forehead on hers.

When our foreheads touched, I forced back the tears and refused to let them spill from my eyes. I wanted to cry for all the life this little innocent would not have, the childhood discoveries, the adolescent joys, the adult accomplishments. All the experiences that made life worth living. I wanted to cry but I would not – I would not.

I was psychotherapist enough to know that my tears would have been not only for her but for myself and my own lost chances. Therefore, I would not cry. I would not be that selfish.

Between the heartbeats hammering at my chest, I sucked in gulps of air and held them in fear because I could see that the baby was not strong enough to breathe for herself.

Then I grew angry, angry at what had been done to this infant and angry at all the selfishness that people had been made to suffer at the hands of parents, siblings and mean-spirited others. Angry for all the deathblows to spirit from teachers and so-called superiors that would cost a painful lifetime to repair. Anger at the needless insults, pointless abuses and exhausting oppositions from thousands of jealous strangers.

And I was angry with that infant's parents for giving me that moment of horror. Angry at my own spirit for bringing me to that place. Angry, angry, angry at my impotence to return that infant to life.

I was so angry that I shook her. Not violently; my anger was not directed at her. But I shook her to wake her up, to call her spirit back from whatever road it was traveling at that moment. I shook her so that she might return to this consciousness and restore my faith in an almighty being who was supposed to look out for the lost, the lonely, for abandoned babies in dumpsters and for burnt-out psychotherapists.

When she didn't stir and my tears wanted to gush around my eyes, I called to her, I begged her through my clenched teeth, "Live! Live!" But she hadn't the strength. She remained lifeless in my hands.

Then from some atavistic knowledge I took a breath and offered it to her. I took the air into my lungs, warmed it with my blood, mixed it with the molecules of my being and offered it to her: I blew gently into her mouth.

Nothing.

"Come on, little one," I whispered. "You know how to do this. Expand your lungs. Take the air."

She didn't move. But I had the feeling, the knowing, that she wanted to.

"I won't hurt you," I promised her, so quietly I could barely hear the words myself. "I'll take care of you." A second time, I passed the breath to her.

No response.

But I was convinced this was going to happen. No god would do this to either one of us, put us this close together just to torment and tease us.

"I didn't create the air, honey," I told her. "It's God's gift to you. It's life! And it's yours! But you've got to take it! Come on, baby! Breathe!"

And for the third time, that spiritual number, that trinity of submission, hope and expectation, I drew in the air and gently blew it towards the baby's face. I said, "Come on, baby! Breathe!"

For a moment I despaired. The little thing hadn't responded, her little lungs didn't expand, her little heart didn't beat. But then I felt a tiny rumble in her chest; like an engine that had been idle for too long, she jolted back to life and began drawing and expelling air.

I watched her for a moment to assure myself that she was really breathing. I watched her delicate nostrils flair and return; I watched her mouth pucker and suck. I watched until I was convinced I was holding a living being.

Then I clutched the new life securely to my breast, whispered words I thought I no longer believed – "Thank You, Lord" – and ran for my Civic.

*

End of this sample.
Enjoyed the preview?
Shamarla will be available for purchase in 2015 from Amazon.com, CreateSpace.com, and other retail outlets, including the publisher: GBSPublishing.com.

This and other titles in the series are available at Amazon.com, Createspace.com, Kindle and many other retail outlets.

Counselor's Couch: Babushka
Counselor's Couch: Gazzara
Counselor's Couch: Lolita
Counselor's Couch: Oscar
Counselor's Couch: Battle of Old Town Hill
Counselor's Couch: Gantry
Counselor's Couch: Maleficent
Counselor's Couch: Book of Shadows
Counselor's Couch: Ilsa
Counselor's Couch: the Wounded Healer

Counselor's Couch

About the Author:

Mr. Stump is a licensed psychotherapist who lives and practices near the coast in southern California. He walks the local beaches and piers regularly but does not meet with clients there. He provides Consultations for Life Transitions via the internet and the telephone.

He particularly enjoys working with interns in order to help the next generation of psychotherapists find its way.

He can be contacted through:
jimstumpcounseling.com.

ALL PRAISE BELONGS TO GOD

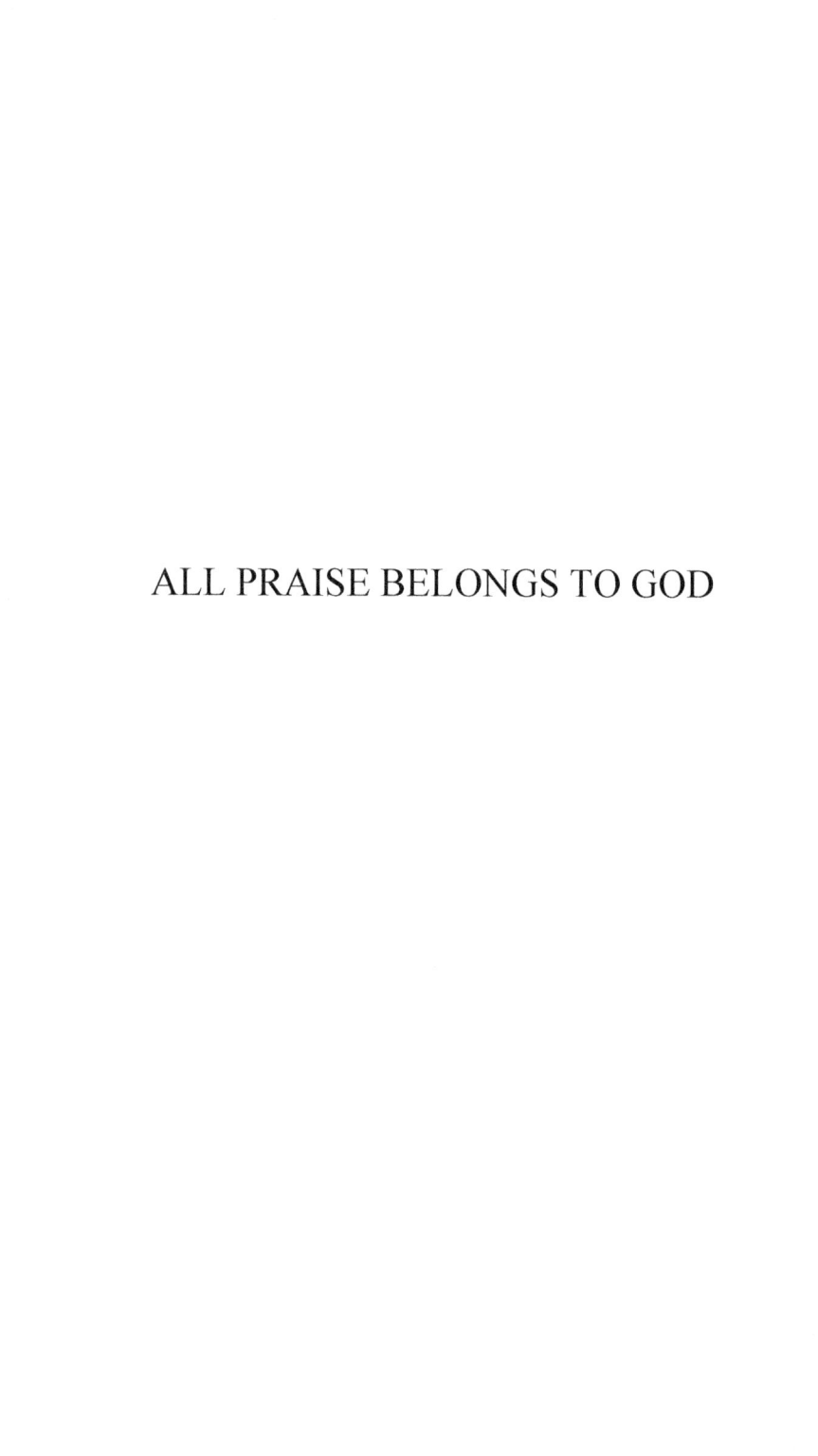

Printed in Great Britain
by Amazon